# Sweet, Sour and Serious

## Survivors' Poetry Scotland

### *Illustrated Anthology*

**SURVIVORS' PRESS SCOTLAND**

Published 10th October 1996 (National Poetry Day & World Mental Health Day)
by Survivors' Press Scotland
c/o Glasgow Association for Mental Health
First Floor, Melrose House, 15/23 Cadogan Street, Glasgow G2 6QQ

A catalogue record for this book is available from the British Library

ISBN 0 9529140 0 X

Edited by Steve Allan, Larry Butler, Helen Crawford, Maggie Graham, Wallace MacBain, Susan Watters, for Survivors' Poetry Scotland

Front cover illustration by Paul Duffus
Majority of illustrations by artists from the Trongate Studios
Typed by Wallace MacBain • Proofread by Peter Manson
Design & typeset by Kevin Hobbes

*Survivors' Poetry Scotland* thanks each of the contributors for texts or illustrations published in this Anthology.

Submission are invited for the second Survivors' Poetry Scotland Anthology and our magazine, first issue scheduled for April 1997.

Submissions are open only to Survivors. A survivor is a person with current or past experience of psychiatric hospitals, recipients of ECT, tranquillisers and other medication, survivors of child abuse, sexual abuse, users of counselling and therapy services, and other survivors who have empathy with our experience, including disabled people.

Poetry, short-fiction or other creative prose and black/white illustrations may be submitted, but not full length novels, although self-contained extracts are acceptable. The work must be neither previously published nor accepted for publication and may be in any of the languages of Scotland.

Please submit no more than six pieces.

Submissions should be typed on one side of the paper only and the sheets secured at the top left corner. Each individual work should be clearly marked with the author's name and address.

Submissions should be accompanied by two stamped addressed envelopes (one for receipt, the other for return of work).

Printed in Scotland by Bell & Bain,
303 Burnfield Road, Thornliebank, Glasgow, G46 7UQ

With support from Glasgow City Council Project Development Fund
And Greater Glasgow Community and Mental Health Services NHS Trust

# SWEET, SOUR AND SERIOUS

# Foreword

I am very honoured to have been allowed to contribute to this anthology. Survivor poets and artists have a special vulnerable viewpoint on reality; they are sensitive to tremors unseen and unheard by others. Because of their own sufferings they are for the most part non-judgemental except sometimes to institutions without feeling. They are alert to the injustices of the world. They write in the persona of others, the drunk, the drugged, the imprisoned, the hopelessly lost. They are at times—and this is best of all— able to write with wonderful humour. They write of suicides and attempted suicides but the paradox of art is that the more it penetrates the storm the less pessimistic the journey becomes. These survivors strive above all for love when there is only a thin veil between them and madness. They find it hard to forget themselves. But poetry and art help, for in the creation of a valuable object, the necessity for form helps to focus as well as to forget. Poetry and art are methods of control but also give disinterested pleasure. And very many poems in this anthology go beyond therapy and the naked cry of pain. They become objects of value, complete in themselves. It is a great privilege to be involved in this work in however small a way. The vulnerable are always with us but so also is poetry. And its insights. And sometimes its gifts of wonder and humour.

Iain Crichton Smith

# Contents

# Introduction

This is the first publication from Survivors' Press Scotland. The first of many we hope. We intend to produce three magazines in a year, an anthology about every two years, and occasional small booklets by individual writers. In the process of editing and publishing *Sweet, Sour & Serious* we learned a lot about what not to do like underestimate how long it will take. Yes we've struggled. We fought. We cried. We pissed ourselves laughing. We lost manuscripts. One of us had a stroke. No one died. No one bought a new car. There were six of us; three women, three men, one car owner, one person with physical disabilities, all of us with first hand experience of receiving mental health services. Only one person with previous experience in publishing. We each read all the contributions several times—giving each contribution a "yes", "no" or "maybe". A contribution with 3 or more yesses was included. We agreed to a maximum of 3 contributions per person. Over 50 writers and 10 visual artists, 94 poems and 30 illustrations are included in the anthology. Contributions came from people living all over Scotland and a few Scots born writers living in England. There was great variety both in content and length. The selection process required more time, effort, and concentration than any of us realised would be necessary. As we proceeded, we had our moments of sadness and frustration as well as real pleasure. For some of us, the poems we most liked were not selected. That disappointment was part of our teamwork (we are still alive, friendly and speaking to each other!) We had some help too from people with professional experience in the world of editing and publishing: Hamish Whyte from the Mitchell Library and former editor of New Writing Scotland; Gerry Loose, writer in residence in South Glasgow and editor of Cutting Teeth; and Kathy Galloway, a Glasgow based writer and editor, who led a workshop for us entitled "The Editor is your Friend". During this workshop we discussed what poetry meant to us and what it might mean to our readers. We agreed on the following goals for the anthology:

• offer a platform for work by survivors, give us a voice

• reduce the stigma and be taken seriously as creative individuals

• to be part of mainstream publications and culture

• to challenge professionals to change attitudes

• to encourage new writing, increase confidence and self-esteem

• to cover its costs, and to sell out the first edition by Christmas

In selecting work to be included in the anthology our editorial values were as follows:

• literary merit • work that doesn't contradict the above goals • equal opportunities for contributors • a good proportion of accessible material • material using different languages and dialects • true feelings • originality • thought-provoking • imaginative • simple • good use of words • appropriate length • does it move me • layout • holds my interest • clarity • visionary •

About a third of this book is made up of illustrations, and most of these images have been produced by members of the Trongate Studios, and these artists went through a similar procedure outlined above. Not everyone's work is included, with no more than 3 illustrations from an individual artist. In selecting the cover design, we invited Alisdair Gray, the writer/ artist of *Lanark* fame, to lend us his professional eye and opinion. Apart from a few images designed with specific text in mind (Jim McCann's photos), any relationship between illustration and poem is purely coincidental.

All the contributors to this anthology are "Survivors".

A Survivor is a person with a current or past experience of psychiatric hospitals, users of tranquillisers, and other medication, users of counselling and therapy services, survivors of sexual abuse, child abuse, drug and alcohol addiction, people with disabilities and other survivors who have empathy with our experience.

Several professional writers have contributed to this anthology. In the history of art and literature, there are many famous people who at some time in their life were labelled "insane" and were given the popular treatment of the day. For many writers on these pages, this will be their first work ever published. Peter Campbell could be described as a professional Survivor, as one of the founder members of Survivors Speak Out from which emerged the first Survivors' Poetry Group in London.

He states:

"We are not only survivors of a mental health system that fails to meet our wants and needs. We are also survivors of social attitudes and practices that exclude us and discount our experience. Many of the identities society would have us assume—the mental patient, the vagabond, the tragic victim of disease—are ones we would never choose for ourselves ...

Through poetry and music, visual arts, writing and action, we must fight for a broader understanding, revaluation of individual experience."

The development of *Survivors' Poetry Scotland* can be seen to enhance the growth of the Scottish user's movement bringing artistic expression to advocacy and empowerment. We are part of a UK wide network of poets, artists, singers, and storytellers promoting a positive voice and image for survivors. Some of our activities on stage and in workshops, may well be therapeutic. Our purpose, however, is quality communication in the form of poems, stories, songs and images, enhanced with music, dance and drama. Our purpose is to celebrate who we are in all our diversities, and to encourage all survivors to come out, and speak out with pride, dignity and beauty. Some of our performances and workshops have included a poem by Tom Osborn, himself a survivor, a former psychiatrist who decided to train as a trapeze artist at the age of 60:

# Ode to Inarticulateness

I want to drink a toast
To the half
Formed thought.
The phrase that gets stuck in the
Throat:
The pause
And.... well.... and....
The stammer
The hiccup
The hum
The er....
The failure of courage
At the last small point
Before the utterance.

That is where most of the words
Of most of us get lost
Most of the time.

And yet we need
Every one of everybody's
Never uttered utterances,
Half-thought thoughts,
Unspoken speeches;
Not necessarily articulated
Into well-made flowing richly metaphored meaningfully
pregnant sentences.
But simply recognised, acknowledged,
Actually utilised.

I resolve (please help me to carry out
My resolution; please; will you resolve also?)
Not to think too much
Or fear

>Or most of all
>Judge too much
>To close my mouth
>And all the many mouths
>On what we want from
>And
>With each other.

11

In editing for the anthology we were struck by the talent and depth of the work submitted—so many people, so many voices with something to say. Writing is such a freeing experience—people's revelations about themselves and how they see the world, their experience of how they live, survive and dream. The anthology offers an opportunity to speak out and be recognised. Gifts to be admired—talents to be applauded.

*Editorial Team:*
*Steven Allan, Larry Butler, Helen Crawford, Maggie Graham,*
*Wallace MacBain & Susan Watters.*

13

# Wee Woman with Two Sticks

You might pass me in the street
and think, a wee woman with two sticks,
and you would never know
of all that I've been through.

A childhood full of trauma.
A marriage been and goner.
The struggle of three kids to raise
and juggling pennies different ways.

Time comes when it catches up,
life gets tough and harder.
As your confidence goes lower
depression then takes over.

You agree to see a psychiatrist
and to go into hospital.
That is when you discover
you've made the worst mistake of all.

The time you spend in there
has you traumatised once more.
And while your children are in care
they're traumatised too while there.

You come out of hospital
with more worries than going in,
but with a strong determination
not to go back there at all.

You struggle for some years
and with your children's troubles cope.
At last you think you're out on top,
then your body health goes flop.

But my mind is free. Yes, free!
So when you pass me in the street
a wee woman with two sticks
is not all you see, you see.

### *Louise McLennan*

# That pleasure

There is a pleasure madmen know
After the bath.
As they stand in the arms of their beltless clothes
And the scrutineers have left the room
With a practised laugh.
There is that pleasure then.

There is a pleasure madmen know
After dusk.
As they search for gods in the pewter skies
And the scrutineer lays down Jane Eyre
Beside his desk.
There is that pleasure then.

There is a pleasure madmen know
Of their kind.
As they embrace by the pot-room door
And the scrutiny of the caring crowd
Has gone blind.
There is that pleasure then.

There is a pleasure madmen know
Without the wine —
That blood and reason hang themselves
On the same line
And the scrutineers dispense love
For the last time.
There is that pleasure then.

(*There is a pleasure sure
In being mad, which none but madmen know!*
—John Dryden)

### Peter Campbell

# Herr Freud and Herr Jung

Freud and Jung went for a piss
in old Vienna Square.
Freud peed higher
then Jung said,
"You really got me there."
A boastful Freud replied,
"I beat you, so I did."
"Maybe so," responded Jung,
"but I'd a problem with my id."

**Susan Watters**

# In the ward

"You'll take it in liquid form," he said.

"But it gives me heartburn."

"Take it."

"No."

He ran towards the dayroom, picked up the bin and jammed it against the door. Four nurses barged the door and a fight broke out. He was pinned to the floor with a fourteen stone nurse sitting on his chest. Another two held his arms. The young nurse pulled his hair downwards. "I can't breathe, can't breathe," he whispered. Suddenly the four pulled him towards the quiet room, pushed him face down on the bed, pulling his trousers and pants down. Swiftly they jammed the needle into his bare buttock and squeezed the syringe fast and hard causing him to cry out. He felt as though he'd been raped. As they left he pulled up his trousers and screamed, "Largactyl makes me stronger."

The End

## Gordon T. Delaney

# Schizophrenia

At her sexual peak
she was a brazen hussy of sorts
dislocated from fellow man
she rinsed candles with blood
from a slit vein.
Not pleasing to the eye
the incubus crouched low
lovingly sipping the fine l'aperitif
her fingers tangled
in his coarse hair pulling
for she was at her sexual peak
not pleasing to the eye
as all sense fixed in delusion
she became an incoherent loner
the perfect bogeyman
for kids next door
as she rinsed candles with blood
from a slit vein
giving life to the lover
who lived in her brain.

*Donna Campbell*

# Memories

The house is full of laughter again. The walls are filled with flowers and birds ( in song. )

The childish wallpaper of rabbits and other "furry friends" has the memories of you listening to "Peter Rabbit" and other Potter tales. These brought to mind many happily filled years.

Our family room is painted lemon, a light and fresh colour. Our outlook is the same; we're glad you've seen the world and are glad that you've decided to return. We've seen your postcards, we've been where you've been, and sampled your fun.

But now, you're home from the "Big Smoke," home from the city. Away from the hustle and bustle of life, and back to the village and gentle village life.

The vase and the flowers, the birds in song, will encourage memories of where you were born. The future looks bright, the future is fun. Memories will stay with you, and we're glad you've come home.

## *Sheila Deane*

# I wish I were supernatural

I wish I were supernatural
I'd fly right thro' the air
I wish I were supernatural
I wouldn't have a care

I'd go to Third Dimension
And travel into time
Straight into the future
I'd make tomorrow mine

I wish I were supernatural
I'd do such crazy things
If I were supernatural
I'd grow a pair of wings

If I were supernatural
I'd chase a tidal wave
Then have some tea with Neptune
Or fight an Indian Brave!

Oh, to be supernatural
It's just a silly dream
But I'd love to be supernatural
It would be such a scream

*Irene O'Neil*

# Torvaig

A solitary, immaculately besuited man
carrying a heavy canvas bag,
paces a gravel platform while
moonlight plays on glistening rails,
tinkling streamlets, distant arm of sea.

Stunted pines shake as an incessant wind
plays a threnody in the telegraph wires
marching beside the railway into the obscurity ahead.

It soothes his mind, this wind, he a stranger from a distant city,
who knows this place so well when summer sunlight
smiles upon those woods and waters all around.

Would that he could abide in this fastness, far from care!
Live out his days as a crofter, but wife and children wait
in Glasgow at the end of the line.

His heartbeat is louder than the rushing of the waters
while scent of pine woods mingles with the acrid tang of seaweed and tar.
The wind scythes throughout his clothes, making him shiver.
Abruptly, the sound of a whistle.

He beholds the train crawling around the next headland,
its headlight piercing the shadows.
Five lighted coaches and two mail vans. The elderly locomotive
is shrouded with escaping steam as her fireman
desperately struggles to keep her on the move. It slows.

The man leaps on board the balcony of the leading coach
dragging his holdall into the gaslit conviviality,
as the guard shouts out the name "Torvaig" and fancies he can hear an echo.

With a whoosh of steam the train pulls away.
Globes of smoke rise between the pines, higher and higher,
dissolving amongst the precipices that fringe the shore.
Its acrid stench spilling far across the shadowy wastes.
Its clatter of wheels diminishing then the murmur of waters becomes louder again.

Suddenly a furry shape scuttles down the platform.
The creatures of the night
retrieve this domain, their home.

## *David Seagrave*

# How the wee fish see it

A bright lit tank is our home
back and forward we dart
round and around we swim
fed once a day that's our lot
round and round the corridor of time
the patients trod one by one
they stop to look at us in the tank

"Poor wee things," they say
"In that tank all day."

Around and around the corridors  they go again
stopping only for dinner or tea
popping pills
sad eyes
depressed state of mind
not a happy face amongst them
when we die the white coats scoop us out
and put us to our heaven down the "Loo"

When they pass out
have they got a heavenly "Loo" too?

*Edward Flanagan*

# That's The Way It Is.

You're unemployed and blue
there are no prospects for you.
People say to me
That's the way it is
Just get on with it

People homeless on the street
no shoes on their feet.
People say to me
That's the way it is
They must get on with it

You are in a lot of pain
You have been let down again
People say to me
That's the way it is
You must get on with it

The world's abused and polluted
people killed and persecuted
People say to me
That's the way it is
Close your eyes to it

Someone out there please try
to say to me
This doesn't have to be.
We all have a right to live
and have a lot to give.
That's the way it is, open your eyes to it.

**_Olive Stark_**

# A patient's life in the day of a psychiatric nurse

Get off that bed!

I don't care if you're tired. Just do
what you're told and get off the bed.

You're not going to leave that bed
in that mess. Straighten it up!

No, you can't go for a walk,
you haven't got a ground pass.

Just go and sit in the day hall
and watch some television.

Don't take that cup into the ward,
you only drink in the day hall.

No, you can't have something for a headache,
the doctor says you haven't got one.

I'm not turning the radio down,
the other patients like it loud.

That doesn't matter, they'll be back soon
and don't you answer me back, madam!

And don't go getting any ideas
about lying on your bed again.

I don't care whether you like it or not,
just eat it!

Switch off that television
and get into bed!

### *Susan Watters*

# The Dream Store

Last night I saw the clouds
as I've never done before
a spiral staircase led me
to a magnificent bulging store.
    Ribbons of dreams in boxes
    lay in waiting for projection
    lovers fleeing in the dark
    looking for love's protection.
Fields of corn,
for children to see
with fairies giving birth
in cushioned oak trees.
    A bridge on a stream
    where trolls hold court
    with poky hats, wigs
    and goats who cavort.
Mountains like Everest
turned upside down
filled with ice-cream
and served by a clown.
    Young children sleeping
    no care of the night
    a cover of wishes
    keeps them snuggled and tight.

*Donna Campbell*

# My child within

My inner being is flamed with fire
A volcano - tempest fuelled.
Anger cascades this human frame
My body aches from wounds—
That hurt sometime past;
But now erupt in pain and anguish.
I can no more suppress you
My child within.

Is this the way to carry a child
To hear you cry?
Not knowing the how of response—
It pains me to hear
The hatred and anger within.
For I who believe so much
In truth and love
Bear deep hurt and sorrow.

As a child I stood silent and still
Peering through a transparent world.
Why did you not see me?
I needed your touch—
I craved your love.
I stood rejected and discarded!
You shamed me—
And laid false guilt upon my soul.

Now this child so lost—
Calls from a depth unknown;
In turmoil seeking love and comfort.
Affection seen but not known—
A love evaded life
Draws attention to a hidden voice.
A lost voice that speaks of need—
I am that child within.

### Helen Crawford

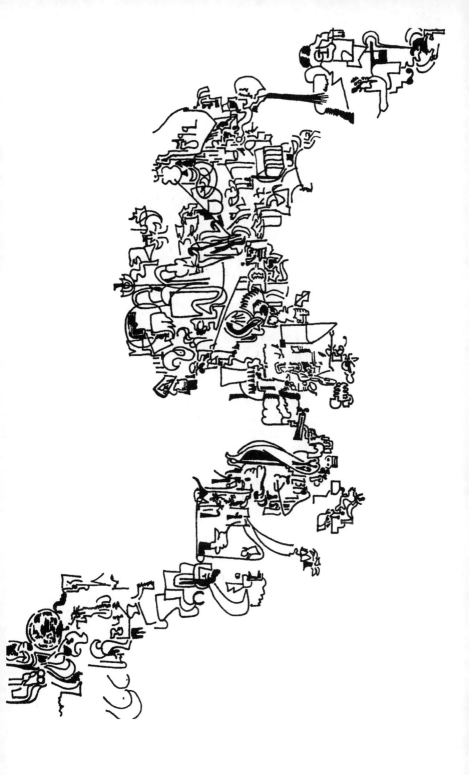

# My Darling is!

The man I love is in a wheelchair,
it doesn't bother me.
I don't care if he can walk,
or uses a chair, I still love him.
I have legs that work,
not very well but they do.
His legs don't, his chair is his mobility
So, that's not his fault.
The problem is you
The problem is you
The problem is you
The problem is you.
He would love to walk again
He gets patronized all the time
by people who are too naive to understand.
He is a good writer
and could go far in this world.

Muscular Dystrophy is his disability.

## *Carrie Palmer*

Dance in harmony tonight
and I'll play the music you like.
Take a break at dawn but not for long

Play with me at the sea and
sing a song along to the sound
of the honey bees buzzing round the trees.

Good morning, the day is dawning
you're an early bird alive and well
your smile mixing with the flowers' smell.

***Michael Allan***

# 3 poems from *a measure*

& we come to a
clear place
picking our way
outside mythology

see the picturesque &
overgrown ruins
of assumptions
see the path now down the hill side
of legacy & geniture

there is time yet   here
to draw breath
& converse

having lifted off   for now
the writhing bestiary we wear
winged   scaled
goat footed & rank

it's a clear view
drink a glass with me
be at ease

**Gerry Loose**

lightning &
though I never moved I
stood on the back of prostrate myth

a fanged carnivore
living in the charnel house
suddenly four

handed with noose
skull stick    blade
& trophy head

there is no escape from time

unmade    unbecome
I wear black holes
my hands recite the prayers

for absenting fear
for that sudden clarity of
unexpected mirrors where

snow falls in the city park like dust
& no one is beside me
no one filling the universe of your place

*Gerry Loose*

& yes death kissed me full    on the lips    teeth    & yes I tried on his
diamante shoes    & yes found him wanting    & yes his drum kit did
not move my feet

she did    she does but    after her is a little death    whose arrogance
drinks with butchers

though time has its own kinesis working its own field    stable    extended
flexible    pliant    a tender city I move over the

line.    I'm leaving mythologies    I only put on wings to please    & my
hooves don't please

it's enough to rattle    my rib cage    click my fingers    dance my own
earthspan dance    unzipped from throat to groin

an ear of corn    an apple falling    a rib removed    I no longer talk in
tongues

## *Gerry Loose*

# Agitation

Agitation, agitation:
I've just reached my limitation.
Pacing up and down the hall,
Bang my head against the wall.
Twitching body, tapping toes -
Out of nothing  nothing grows.
Mutter, mutter, biting lips,
Tremor in my fingertips.
Pulse is racing, eyesight blurred,
Mouth is dry and tongue all furred.
Agitation, agitation;
Heart, please stop your palpitation.

**_Jill McLeish_**

# An other spirit

Willie and Johnny were workmates and pals for over 40 years through thick and thin. Johnny died suddenly, Willie was left all alone, he took to booze with a vengeance.

"O why, O why did wee Johnny die?"

Drink was his only Pal now.

Staggering home with a belly full of booze and a head full of 'Shite'. Coming to the path of his house thumbing through his pockets for his keys, he found that the door was open before he put the key in the keyhole. Going into the livingroom, Johnny was sitting on his favourite chair.

"You're dead, I can see right through you. You're a Ghost!"?

" Yes Willie I have passed over I am in the Spiritual World. I've come to see that you can get back into the Spiritual way of life before you pass over."

"BUGGER OFF! you didn't think of me when you died. I've a new Pal noo he's 'Wee Johnny Walker' and in the best of Spirits and going for over two hundred years. Am away doon fur a couple o mair haufs and I'll be in Heaven tae night."

"That's wit you think,"

### *Eddie Flanagan*

# Aunty's an uncle's

See ma uncle
see when ih grabs mi
an throws mi ower iz knee
an slaps ma bum
an sits me up
an rubs iz jaggy beardy
face ower mine
see ma aunty
shi jist laughs

*Cecilia Grainger*

# Being seen

So you think you see me
you can't see me not really
you only pretend to see me
it's all in your imagination
no one ever sees me    I hide
even out in the open    I'm an
invisible shadow safely camouflaged
like a pheasant sitting on her eggs
no one will ever see me or will they

Will I let you see me    who sees me
sees    nothing    will I give you permission
to see me    completely    what do I fear
being found out    what will you find out
perhaps there's nothing to me    you'll look
and look and look and you'll see nothing

there's nothing to see
I don't exist    I pretend
to be here but I'm elsewhere    absent
unborn disembodied skirting the galaxy
I float in a time warp of faded memory
searching for another world

*Larry Butler*

# Ben Sgulaird

I was wrought by the torments of glaciers in a far-off time,

Before your kind,

Evolved your mind

My rockstuff spilling

Down rivulets, tumbling

To my engirdling sea.

Purposeful little climbing-creature, I have need of thee.

Stand proud upon my topmost crag from whence the eagle soars

Survey and understand

What forces shaped the land

Behold the cloud-armadas glide

High o'er my dappled moors.

Seed of the Almighty!  Here dissolving

Into a greater Totality,

Be thou my guardian, my friend!

Pledge to keep me holy,

Clean as the driven snow.

Safely, homeward go

To thronged agora where thy brethren meet,

And to them, speak.

Be pilgrims, returning,

Gather here, rejoicing,

All voices blending,

In joy never ending.

*David Seagrave*

# Best behaviour

I must be good.  I must be good, and not disturb
the neighbourhood.
I must try to go unnoticed—attention on me
can't be focused.
The staff must think that I'm OK
So they'll ignore me through the day
I must find a true solution,
Preventing deserved retribution.
Maggots must not pass my lips—
Death or smell—I can't make slips.
I must be on my best behaviour
And from this vow I must not waver.
They mustn't think I seek attention
So these dire things I dare not mention.
I mustn't talk about the knife
I dream will soon extinguish life,
Or mutilate and cut and maim
And cause excruciating pain.
I must be good. I must be good, and not disturb
the neighbourhood.

### *Jill McLeish*

# Caring

I care about the world's people.
I care about Mum and Dad.
I care about the leaky church steeple.
I care about an unhappy marriage.

I care for all the world's children.
I care for my brother and sisters.
I care for the memories they all had
I care for life's times, to be glad.

If I ever stop caring,
I'm sure hoping not deliberately.
But hoping, it's just the end of the wearing and tearing,
of each and every 'hard' day.

I care enough to think it.
I care enough to say.
But most of all, I care enough to let you know this way.

If you care enough to read this,
then don't stop there I say.
'Cos you'll go on in life with the wisdom,
to care enough to pray.

**James Anthony Daly**

# Chemical escape

Shi looked it thi boatul

Shi picked it up

Shi opened it

Shi emptied it oan thi table

Shi coonted 160 pills

Shi spread thum oot

slid thum roond aboot

feelin thur energy

thur buzz, thur control, thur powur

powur ti take hur intae fluid city

shuttin oot grotsville, cuttin oaf torture town.

Shi scooped up thi pills

slowly

an started pittin thum

back in thi boatul

*Cecilia Grainger*

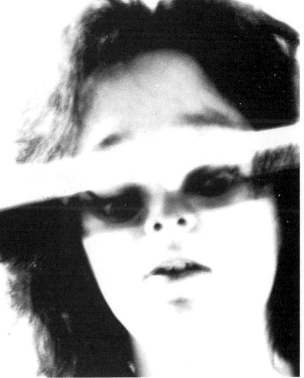

# The bin

I rest the bin
on the stone wall.
O not eternal
the midnight black urn.

So it will turn
idly through the dark
till in the dawn
in the din of the lark
the men will lift it,

my midnight black urn,
my lightweight vase,
my plastic bin.

It tilts into the red
clouds of the dawn
which are like iron,

my lightweight bin
which is not eternal
but carries the waste
of a transient past.

**_Ian Crichton Smith_**

This Verse I've Written For My Little Niece Santina

# My Little One

When I see my little one, I always know she's alright
I kiss and hug and hold her tight, and hope she has sweet dreams at night
She's growing fast, and she's so bright
Oh little one, stay in my life

She always remembers, when we've forgot
I can't believe her little thoughts
And when she speaks, it's such a delight
Oh little one, you're so nice

And when I leave, oh little one
I laugh so much, and then I smile
For one so young, so sweet  and gay
You're so special, in a funny way.

Love you always
Aunty Marilyn
To My Angel
xxx
xxx
x

## *Marilyn Donald*

# Dawn

The night is gone, a new day breaks.
Who knows just now what steps man takes?
All is quiet and slow and calm
no breeze to break the silent balm
of dawn.

It is now one thinks of things anew,
of all one's plans and hopes, tho' few
of them will come to any close,
since it is false - this rose
of dawn.

It is a time when all seems fresh,
like new born babes lying in creche -
so tender and small, yet soon to grow
into men - hard and big and not so slow
as dawn.

Man begins his day again,
out into the world - his prison pen.
To eat and sweat and toil -
at work he does not wish to soil
his hands, because they are tied -
tied to himself.

It is easy to say "Awake at dawn"
and not put your thoughts into pawn.
Put them to that use you really wish
to do this day.  Make full use of this swish
of dawn.

It is harder to carry on tho', throughout the day
as pressures come to bear and make you say
those things you disbelieve and do these things
that need not doing because they are born after the wings
of dawn.

Let Dawn come and go, and wait awhile
until you are able to really smile
at yourself and the world and all mankind.
It takes time to really find
a new dawn.

**Eric Davidson**

# Death

Sky, colours of Dutch tiles,
a loch reflects the sun
and pines crest the horizon
rocking the osprey nests.
My search pierces the planet,
winds round the universe,
finds a resting place within.
Gratitude for having lived,
for having known such beauty,
warms the images of death
that dance through these days.

*Kay Carmichael*

# Doctor, you fascinate me

Doctor, You fascinate me
I wonder why
You always sit with your legs crossed;
When you were a child
Did your mother tell you it was rude
To have them splayed?
I wonder why your socks are not odd;
Are you expressing some subconscious desire
To identify with the man in the street?
And is it due to
An obsessional fear of cancer
That you do not smoke?

How much time we waste
On my mundane problems
When you are a much more
Interesting case!

### *Joanna McFarlane*

# Gatecrashers!

Doubting Thomas came one day
to keep William Worry at bay.
Then Cynical Sally came around before I
went to bed.
They all had a party in my head.
Then I came along again & threw them out.
"Until the next time" they did shout!

**Olive Stark**

# Geographies of love

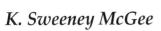

Moving
in and out of love
cruising coastlands
scanning interiors
reaching the rimland
searching for the core
the heartland
again
out on the periphery

geographies of love
dreams of love
waking love
shifting love
waiting for love
voicing distinctions
making endless changes
living out the years
what love is

sea change
small rain falling
rivers running
reservoirs filling
leaping   living
channels of
boundless
equal love
artesian brimming
held now
at rest
I place a signifier
a fountainhead
a witness to my ground
my well
my heart

*K. Sweeney McGee*

# How can a woman learn to love a man?

Fucked by her father
Regularly, relentlessly.
Saturday night fever:
Boys boozing
Macho mating
Pass the parcel—
Tiny toddler.
Body stimulated
Mind bewildered
Feelings frozen;
Paralysed panic
Locked into body cells.
Programmed by the past
To love that never lasts;
To the paralysed panic
Of the tiny toddler's tortured
Ecstasy.

Our father who art in heaven—
Then who the hell is this, here on earth?

How can a woman learn to love a man
When she's programmed by the past
By men who, filled with drunken lust
Would take her tiny toddler's body
Play with it in thoughtless revelry.
Baby then, couldn't talk, couldn't move
Too young to know, too young to tell
How many years of living hell
Are locked inside
Too scared to tell, too scared to yell

Survival demands forgetting
Except at night-time, dreamtime sweating
And the legacy held in every cell
Holds the body stiff.
Whenever body stimulated—
Feelings frozen, mind bewildered
Locked—forever?—in paralysed panic.

### Leonie FitzGerald

# Dark room

It is dark when I enter the room
my hands search for a switch

UP

DOWN

LEFT

RIGHT

NOTHING!

I cannot find one!
I stand still
not wanting to move
any further into the dark
until I have some light.
I check my pockets
I have no matches or a lighter
I start to sweat!!
I am afraid of the dark.
I take a step backwards,
to leave this
Dark Room.

But!
The door has closed.
I tremble!!!
Panic strikes!!!
I fumble for the handle,
I find it.
I pull.
It does not open.
I am alone.
Trapped!
in
this
**Dark Room.**

## *Wallace MacBain*

## Me

THE ROOM WAS QUIET,
I WALKED OVER TO THE MIRROR
TO SEE IF I WAS THERE,
BUT NO, THERE WAS SOMEBODY ELSE
THEY LOOKED BACK, I STARED,
I DIDN'T RECOGNISE MYSELF
MY OWN REALITY HAD STARTLED ME.
FEAR SHOT THROUGH ME,
JOLT OF BLOOD PRESSURE, PANIC, SHAKING.
HOLD ONTO THE CHAIR, CLOSE MY EYES,
BLANK MY MIND, BREATHE SLOWLY,
WALK AWAY.

### *Sadie Ashcroft*

# The anvil of love

We are shaped young
on the anvil of love.
The furnace is there
in our mother's arms
and our molten lines
take form with her milk.

Gentle flames lap the cradle,
weave a lattice as we grow.

Fire flares again,
melting base metal
liquid gold.

The hammer strikes
again, again.

We are shaped young
on the anvil of love:
a bitter-sweet pain
which never ends,
as the hammer rings
again, again.

**Anne Marr**

I live on the edge
of madness.
Only a membrane
fine as silk
weaves between my self
and inner caves
where pain and terror lurk.
Behind that skin,
sometimes seen by
my unfocussed eye,
a creature lives,
not mine, but bound to me
in old familiar ways, altering my vision
of the world.
Today the membrane ripped
and loosed not only him
to rampage through my head
but others I should have
killed off long ago
had I known how
had you been there to help.

*Kay Carmichael*

# The One Picture
# (An Aon Dealbh)

The flashing lightning rent the vault of sky
And, as a serpent's tongue,
Extended a finger through my window
Leaving behind a thousand fragments
In place of the one mirror
And, in place of the one face
I was watching before me,
A thousand pictures.

Sickness of mind tore the firmament of my being
And, as the poisonous sting of the serpent,
Extended a finger into my soul
And left behind
In place of one person a thousand diseased
fragments
Shouting and warring with each other
Like legions of hell.

In the name of compassion
Rescue and relieve my soul
Before it is forever destroyed;
Extend your hand in through the window,
My spouse, my brother, my sister,
Restore music to my silent heart
Blow the breath of your mouth into my nostrils,
Revive me and to me restore
The One Picture

### *Rev. Roderick MacDonald*

# An Aon Dealbh
# (The One Picture)

Reub an dealannach boillsge an iarmailt
Is mar theanga na nathrach shin e
Meur a steach air an uinneig
Is dh' fhag e, 'n a dheidh,
An ait aon sgathan, mile spealg,
Is, an ait na h-aon aghaidh
A bha mise coimhead fa mo chomhair,
Mile dealbh.

Reub tinneas na h-inntinn iarmailt mo chre
Is mar ghuin nimheil na nathrach shin e
Meur a steach ann am anam
Is dh' fhag e 'n a dheidh
An ait aon phearsa mile bloigh coirbt'
Is iad ag glaodhaich is ag cogadh an aghaidh
A cheile, mar Legion an Iutharn.
An ainm an t-sealbh—

Dean cobhair is fuasgladh air m' anam
Mus teid gu siorruidh cli e;
Cuir do mheur a steach air an uinneig,
Mo cheile, mo bhrathair, mo phiuthar,
Is aisig ceolraidh do m' chridhe balbh,
Seid anail do bheoil a m' chuinneanan,
Is thoir beo mi, is dhomh aisig
An aon dealbh.

### *Rev. Roderick MacDonald*

# The papers

Popping out in the morning
getting away from the heat
to breathe in good fresh air
when we walk along the street

Cut down on Albert Drive
to the Paper Rack
where we get my daily newspaper
so we're standing at the lights

Crossing busy main road
as the green man flashes
we walk on up the pavement
safe as bricks in these grand houses

## *Bobby Christie*

From an idea by *Arnold Manuel*

# Isn't it great

LOOK AT ME, ISN'T IT GREAT

LOOK AT THIS, ISN'T IT GREAT

THIS WAS FREE, ISN'T IT GREAT

I WAS HELPING MY MUM, NOT SO GREAT

SHE SAYS. "YOU'RE A GOOD LAD, THAT'S GREAT

SO I'LL BUY YOU SOME CRISPS, THAT'S GREAT

SPACE INVADERS MUM, THAT'S GREAT

THERE'S A FREE GIFT MUM, THAT'S GREAT

JUST LOOK WHAT IT IS, ISN'T IT GREAT.

### *Jim McCann*

# Moving my mind

My mind is whirling
It's all too much
There's too many things to consider
I have to decide
I have to take action
They're depending on me to deliver!
Should I do THIS
What about THAT
And the NEXT THING is coming up soon
Here's someone else
With a problem to share
Oh God - I feel like a "goon"
I've got to escape
Shut myself off
Have a good cry in the loo
But it's really no use
It won't go away
There's only one thing I can do
Dead-march to the bus
Head bending down
So no-one will see the tears
Get home fast
Lock the front door
Collapse and give in to my fears
Panic is coming
I can't think straight
I'm hot and I'm sore - I feel ill
Horrible thoughts
Of guilt and remorse
Attack me from all angles still
I close everything down
Shut everything off
Collapse in an unfeeling heap
In between tears
And mindless fatigue
Are periods of restless sleep

Daylight has come
Don't want to get up
Don't care if I live or die
But "something inside"
Says "Oh yes you do -
Though right now you can't understand why"
Well I won't get a coffee
Or light up a fag
Unless I get moving from here
Then the folk at the pub
Will think I have "gone"
And they'll bloody well drink all the beer!
Well I'm not having that
So get out of my way
Clothes and some dosh I will find
I somehow feel better
Got back my old self -
It's all about

MOVING MY MIND!!

*Betty MacKintosh*

# Mr Freud Mr Freud
# How do you do

I am the sleepmaker. The Rocker. Singer of lullabys.
Dream Maker. Dress Maker. Safe Cracker. Beside this,
before this, is this not poetry. Yes I am poetry (first
foremost tasteless classless fast food thoughtless stuff)
and I lick all the sons and daughters goodnight after
repeating endlessly the same words in the same drone.
At the end of each verse, I clone images of unknowable
events into the sleeper's skull until the headless wanderer
creeps in their blood.

I travel alone, stay nowhere, never sleep, am part of every
thing, I am the one who:   pulls out your teeth

> rapes your mother
> murders your father
> grows a penis
on your sister's cunt
cuts off your balls
chases you along cliff edges

shoots, stabs, pokes, clobbers,
I climb into your womb, eat your child
stir turds in your soup,
I am the whore in your husband's head,
the secret you will never know.
your wife's lover with bloody slobber,

I live on the mountain of delight
above the valley of terror.

I am guilty guilty guilty of every horrible thing ever done or
imagined but your children love me, the insane know me as a
friend, the diiing embrace me. I am ever young always awake
always with you, so when you see me, laugh and look at my blood
red tongue. Kiss me, I have no clothes   no skin, lick my guts
and I will sing.

*Larry Butler*

# Job search

When writing CVs, be SUCCINCT:
Not trite, polite; brief, not NAIF.

Don't use the daisy-wheel
Typeheads - employers hate them:
And don't let your house style
Reveal your mean speed
Is five words a minute
Picked out with painful
SLOWNESS

       Should you make it
To the interview, be deferential,
Not OBSEQUIOUS: don't contradict yourself,
Answer as many questions as possible
Without actually LYING.

If appointed, express
Gratification, not amazement.

However harassed, try to stick it out
For at least a fortnight.

Failing that, take a ticket
To Samoa or Siam,
Or a long walk
Off a short pier.

*A.D. Foote*

# from Siren Song

between the twilight
and the dusk
who will hold me
in their loving arms

alchymical marriage
over
union of opposites
complete
Siva and Shakti
become one
in the twilight
and the dusk
who will hold me
in their arms

he-dyke
eunuch at the temple of Aphrodite
*I heard woman song*
mirror of me
brave fool enough
to grasp the lightning rod
and follow through
through
into Aphrodite's night

when morning comes
and the mist has cleared
my heart a shallow grave
who will hold me then
when morning comes

### K. Sweeney McGee

# Yet again

Night ends with a dawn chorus.

But the moon
Is in tune
With no one.

A spider spins in the corner.

The light is
As sweet as nectar
Or the scent
From your dear
One's skin.

Morning engines start running.

Shattered
Your dream of paradise.

Now to rise
And face the hate and lies
Of yet another day.

The very thought
Is chilling.

**_Jack Withers_**

# keeping time

time is essential
when we're riding our bikes
timing is essential
when cycling our bikes

keep an eye on kerb stone
strike a fine straight line
as our wheels spin round
we speed into the future

with grins on our faces
breaking away from city scape
till we're on the edge of country
green grass fields and clean air

when cycling our bikes
timing is essential
when we're riding our bikes
how free it is to be alive

*Bobby Christie*

# Monsieur Michel

I fell in love with him two weeks before I saw him. His image had been forming in my mind and was gaining substance with each approaching day.

He would certainly be beautiful. After all, he was a man, he was French and I was twelve; teetering on the edge of teenagedom. Of course, he would be beautiful.

There I was, all parcelled up in the straightjacket of convent school, where the only males to be encountered were a psychopathic physics teacher and a couple of aging priests; oh.... and also... the boys from St. Aloysius. There were lots of them, and within spitting distance, but they were strictly out of bounds. Our nuns carried out daily lunchtime raids on the cafe between the two schools. Wimples billowing, they pounced, ousting every female slow enough not to have seen them coming. A solid thwack from a wooden rosary was always available to counter any foolish resistance.

Then, there was the weekly lecture in the Assembly Hall, on the dire consequences of fraternising with the boys from St. Aloysius. It was many years before I dared ask anyone what fraternising meant. So, the announcement of a male student from France coming for a term was greeted with no small amount of anticipation. I barely ate the week before the start of term. My best friend, Anne, however, proudly declared her dislike of Frenchmen and loyally stated that she had no intention of marrying any other than a British citizen. Less competition for me to worry about then.

The day duly arrived. As did Monsieur Michel, late. Too late for me to see him before I had to make my way to Biology. An agonising two days elapsed before I got my first glimpse of him. The long awaited encounter was no more than a passing blur in the hallway. Still, he was taking my French class the very next day...

I loved learning French but the only subject I studied that afternoon was the vision unfolding before my eyes; and ears, for it was his voice that really kindled my hormones. Lulled by the soothing sensuality of that sultry accent I swept in and out of consciousness. Lost in a reverie of village squares, boulangeries and patisseries I drifted through the class on a cloud. When he complimented me on my French accent it was all I could do to keep from slithering to the floor.

Alas, this happy state of affairs was not to continue. After only one more lesson with him he was transferred to the opposite half of the curriculum. I was destined to never hear those melodious tones again.

For the remainder of term I pined for my Monsieur Michel. He had, indeed, come to be known as mine for I had set up quarters at the gate, monitoring his every coming and going. I became a very familiar lunchtime sight (the St. Aloysius boys long ago relegated!). In all weathers I stoically took up my post, hoping to snatch a peek at him. It was my only chance of seeing him, and I did, a few times. My broken little heart, however, eventually succumbed to the inevitable, his imminent departure from our shores.

I called out to him one day before he left,
"Bon voyage, Monsieur Michel!"
"Merci, Susanne," came the reply.
He remembered my name! He remembered my name....

This then was my Monsieur Michel; and was he beautiful? In all truth, he had a face like a sucked in balloon. But what did that matter. He was French, and I was twelve.

## *Susan Watters*

# Letting go

Letting go,
of the water that wets me
thoroughly cooling,
that chills me reducing
the glow where it grows.

letting go,
of the anger that pains me so
and bids me do and be
the hateful thing that in
pretence is styled as
unassailable justice
for an absolute ending.

Letting go,
then there would be nothing
to show for all the efforts;
all the pains and shames
that have remained.

Letting go,
of the imagined hurt
that is harder to bear
because of the place
where it is felt.

Letting go is never easy
that is why we fear to die
because then there is no way
to be afraid to let go;
because then there is
no way to hold on;
only letting go.

**Dominic Boyle**

# Morning

Morning
lifts its covers
off the hills.

The horizon line
is clear again
and instead
of holding
tight
to fear

I flow
and hear once more
the lightness
of dancing souls.

All this
because I choose
to change my mind

and Love
in kind

responds.

***Jinty Brooke***

# Excerpt of "Erotomania"

Entered my life by the screen, he did. That's how we met, you see. Twenty-six I was and he was just... just himself. Anyway, we passed our thoughts and intense emotional energy to each other through the T.V. waves. I wanted him. He *was* mine and he wanted *me.*

I recall the sheer adoration of his physique and of the person I knew. Yes, I knew him so well. He knew *me.*

**HE LOVED ME, YOU SEE.**

Bending to flick my cig in the ashtray, he made the date—"I'll see you at two" was the whisper.

"TWO", I THOUGHT, "YES, TWO".

I screeched, making no sound; an accompaniment: the flurry of passion, the gripping love in my belly.

"I'll see you at two", I whispered.

EXHAUSTED NOW. MUST SLEEP.

I was ready at two, eager, restless, excited...

But, as the minutes ticked by, I refused the pills, I refused the liquid. So, they began to remove "him" with one of their injections.

## *Janice Eadie*

# Little

I like little
It's safety
But I fuckin'
Can't stand
Smallness
Those clean nails
And little hands
Keeps that child
Safe
Wrap it up in bigness
The nakedness
Feels safe
But the blindness
Of power
Makes us rape
The littleness
The nakedness
The beauty
In each and
Every one of us.

**Maggie Cameron**

# Requiem to our fallen trees

On twenty fourth October
In the year of Ninety Five
A gale arose of such a force
It downed some trees to die.

Many of our bonny trees
Succumbed to the wind that night
And in the light of dawn next day
I surveyed the sorry sight.

Their beauty filled my eyes for years
When in Spring they came to leaf.
I revelled in their greenery
While children played beneath.

I looked upon them on the grass
With sadness in my eyes.
This ode is worded in their honour
And sorrow at their demise.

### *Louise McLennan*

# Institution:

In our institute
Our boss was astute

As well as being a brute

Hatred and fear became the
 order of the day

No one was in the union
So we turned to religion
In a kind of a way
And began to pray for that day
When the swine may resign
And hopefully go away
Then Hallelujah one day he did
But not a single one of us
Spat down
On the coffin-lid
For we weren't at the funeral
As we had a free day

*Jack Withers*

# Transpersonal hospital dance

free falling goblins lurk
in the shadows between wards
flying like bats down long corridors
falling from grace they dive into the lucky dip
free at christmas finding a timid new nurse
on duty for her first brace zealous and over
pragmatic with alacrity she gives her best boot
to her patients while jealous green goblins giggle
in dark corners shove bedpans under her feet
till she free falls down the laundry chute

*Larry Butler*

one's beliefs
    one's iceberg
one's sanity
    one's storage room
one's thoughts
    one's bookmarker
one's mind
    one's bird cage
one's life
    one's toilet
one's philosophy
    one's university
one's hospital
    one's music

### *Pedro Keldro*

# The One

I Have Been There
The Place Where
All Was Gloom
And No Light Shone.

I Have Climbed Out
Struggled Upright
Glimpsed The Sun
Gave A Glad Shout.

I Have Dwelt In
The Place Where
Death Is Near
And Hope Was Dim.

But I Trusted
In The One
Who Gives Life
And Life Began.

Here I Am.

### *Louise McLennan*

# Prison is my home

Home is my prison
I am a prisoner of circumstance
Society has tolerated my
Existence throughout my life
Now I tolerate society.

No more to walk in dark shadows for
They cannot protect me any more
Society within society cannot protect me for
I must be a prisoner who has to pay for
No crime, apart from his own
Prison shall eat me—
Prison shall waste me—
Prison can make me hate—
Prison can make me into a monster
But society has already done that.

Prison is my endearment
Endearment is my prison
Stepping back, stepping inward
Society and prisoner no more
It is either Yes or No, there can be no
Indecisiveness in my
Prison.

Prison is my Home
Home is my Prison.

## G. Higginbotham

# If...

If butterflies could talk,
they would tell us how beautiful they looked.

If elephants did not produce ivory,
then lesser animals would not murder them.

If the clouds could be manipulated,
then famine would become a thing of the past.

If people cried when they should have done,
then the world would be a better place.

If people took me more seriously than they do,
then I would be half the man I am now.

If every picture told a story
then the smaller things in life
would receive the attention they deserve.

*Stephen Allan*

17/8/95

# Sadness

In the midst of darkness
a small warm light appears
little sobs of sadness
crystal drops of tears
Her lover died of cancer
Her mother died of Aids
All she has left in life
is jewels of different shades.

A candle can bring warmth
A candle can bring love
A love triangle comes
But her life is torn to pieces
She may never smile again
Her love for him she will always have
Her tears seem to never end.

**Carrie Palmer**

# KBP3

I have been standing here for some time now
watching the ensuing battle with only a passing interest
as the advantage shifts from my neighbouring comrades
to the menacing advances of a similar enemy.
Occasionally the rising smog will disperse
allowing creative tactics to be examined in full.
*But despite it all, I know I will fall.*

Frustration grows at my lack of control and choice
as I await inevitable orders from he who never cared.
With only a slow advance in the one direction
and never the option to surrender or retreat
I stand before a strategic nightmare riddled with uncertainty
with my only purpose being to protect the protected.
*It's occurring to me why; I'll eventually die.*

My alter-ego approaches into my surrounding space
with a menacing sneer and his sword held high
little does he realise the support I uphold
as the horseman prevents his futile attempt
to strike at the heart of my brave patriots.
So am I this expendable with my lowly status.
*Or does someone actually care; over this petty affair.*

At last the order to advance is finally issued
and all eyes from both sides turn in my direction
as I walk cautiously into uncharted territory
wondering why such a privilege is bestowed upon me
when most of my defences have not even flinched.
But suddenly my bravery turns to nervous fear.
*Am I awaiting a fate; that's probably come late.*

The seconds tick by and the tension mounts
as another two fall to my right without complaint.
Then the loneliness engulfs me and paranoia prevails
and with sudden dread I hear a roar from afar
of a man twice my size who charges towards me
*with an order to destroy my very existence.*

*But then again,*
*I knew all along,*
*That I was only a pawn.*

**Stephen Allan**

# Multi-Faceted

I like to dress up
In other people's lives
And be what I am not:

The fresh-faced kid
With sports shirt and baseball cap
Chewing gum and washing people's cars
On the block;
The professional something or other
Lunching with clients
In neatly tied back hair
And with brief-case in hand;
The monocled aristrocrat
Entertaining in his parlour
With spotty cravat
And silk smoking jacket;
The well-oiled intellectual
Bespectacled and open-neck shirted
Smoking roll-ups in some seedy cafe

When I change back into my own clothes
I can't find myself in the mirror
It must be hard
Keeping up with an empty space like me

*Joanna McFarlane*

# Journey

Up first

I went in the wrong direction

and
the bicycle did the same

Then I went down
But down and then along

Crash
onto
the ground

Ground is a soft word
it was hard hard hard
edge in my shoulder
what happened
where am I
I'm...

Back on the earth
solid on the ground
I think, I feel I think I think I feel, I feel me think
but bits of me are missing

I'm not all together

I don't want to be there because it's a road
but I do because what else to do.

I feel so silly

what happened

down here

My legs crawl up towards me
and push me up
but they don't

I HURT HURT HURT HURT HURT HURT

I can see

But something is strange
funny shapes, flickering all around
and not together
The world                              what shall I do
is                                     I must get home

jumbled
fractured            my arm won't move
mixed                     oh yes it does in one
                              D
                              i
                              r
                              e
                              c
                              t
                              i
                              o
                              n

This has so completely
never before but happened

                                        The world broken up
                                        edges the at still is

My legs push again
then work
I feel
I'm here

What now

I walk
jelly
red jelly
jelly legs
jelly eye
red jelly eye

I ride
I wobble of
          f.


*Morwyn Porter*

# Sedated

She had slept for twenty hours
When we heard the door of her room
Click open
In her night-dress
She staggered through a blanket of hair
Behind which
The pallor of her aging face
Was broken
By two heavy sunken eyes

At the end of the corridor
She hesitated
Before stumbling into the Duty Room
As the door closed behind her
The pleading began
But resolutely they shook their heads
She responded in a barrage of weary moans
And dragged her arm
Over the contents of their desk
Coffee-filled mugs smashed
As they hit the floor
And ink-smudged case notes
Were tossed into the air
At the window
We saw her press her contorted face
Against the glass, which shuddered
As her fists beat down on it
With a heavy grip on her arms
They managed to drag her out of sight
Leaving only a trail of saliva on the glass

With jacket now off
And sleeves rolled up to the elbow
He raised the syringe
And judged its contents with steady eye

After a while
The whimpers had begun to fade
And the rocking of the chair slowed
to a steady halt
When all was quiet
We resumed our game of dominoes

## *Joanna McFarlane*

# See You

SEE YOU THERE

DO YOU KNOW A SECRET

OR DO YOU HAVE SOME INFO

HAVE YOU CRACKED IT

ARE YOU SURVIVING

AND IT'S ME THAT'S DYING.

*Jim McCann*

# Skippered

I sit alone on the street, nae money tae get food
Hunger is starting tae pain ma belly
I tak a sip fae a bottle o' Whiskey
I used tae hate booze, but times are hard
I drink Whiskey when I can afford it
Cans o' Super Lager or whatever the rest o' the time
People despise me as they go past
I hear their harsh comments:

"He should not be allowed out on the street."
"It is a bad image for Glasgow."
"Nobody should get into that state."
"He should be locked up."

It is no ma fault, I worked hard fae years
Then I wiz made redundant, couldnae find anither job
I got intae debt, and lost ma hoose then pit oot on tae the street
I stayed in Homeless Hostels fir a while
I started tae drink tae tak the depression awa
Before long I wiz an Alki, drinking ma Giro in a couple o' days
Tapping other Alki's or begging in the street
I just hud tae huv a drink
Kipping in shop doorways or on Park benches
Cause I couldnae walk hame
I am so drunk I huv pissed ma troosers
I am tae drunk tae stan' up, I fall in a heap
Smashing the bottle in ma pocket
I swear at people as they go by:

"Whit are ye bastards lookin' at?"
"Can I no huv a wee drink in peace?"

God! I'm a complete mess, so I shout obscenities at ma self:

"Ya silly bloody eejit. Whit the fuck are ye gonna do noo?"

Somebody has called the Polis, they tak me to the cells
Lock me up fir the night, I leave sober in the mornin'
Go and cash ma Giro, start all over again
Will it ever end so I can huv a life once mare
Or am I tae remain a doon'n oot forever?

**_Wallace MacBain_**

# Shattered Dreams

I hear your hollow laughter, as well as hear your sighs of secret pain. I too pretend and invent to hide my own secret shame. I too wear plastic smiles and faces to hide the tears by day, but not by night while alone. The emptiness of my world of empty friends and visitors, the places I cannot go.

The total emptiness of my heart is confusing. It all magnifies my own fears to a point that I can no longer hide my fears and tears, but hide them I must.

I can understand how it feels to be alone day in, day out, I've been running from loneliness for the last ten years. You ask who will take your burden, and wrap loving arms around you, to give your heart a home? I took that same question, then ran and ran, I'm still running, while I ask that question.

I struggle like you every day, and try so hard to win, I cry out each night with a heavy heart, it is my pillow that dries my tears at night, I know that isn't right.

I too long for happiness, but until I find my home, I cannot give my heart a home it dearly needs, and like yourself, I too ask, who will give my heart a home

## *G. Higginbotham*

# Sea

These waters would kill me.
Only fish can survive
in that boiling inferno
or you can see a bird dive
into a salty furrow.
Roof after roof collapses
of transient slaty houses
and suddenly the white horses
rear hoof after hoof
beating the sky away.

*Ian Crichton Smith*

# The Garden

The tangled garden of my dreams,
I could bring to you.
I could show you, rain-beaded,
A spider's web of hope,
Trapping early sun.
A crazy path that curls through bowers,
Where spiky roses reach their hungry hands,
And tumbled ivy on the wall
Spills over the bruised moss.
I could tell you my desires,
And wrap the flawed net of my hopes
Around us both.
But you would run from the wilderness,
Wanting an ordered, Italianate space,
Empty, and without me.

### *Anne Marr*

# Petals

Rose petals fall to the ground.
I gaze at the pattern -
Feel the soft velvet fragility
And stroke the curved shape
A petal - part of an entire beauty
An individual rose in fragments.
The wind blows - lifting and
Scattering the velvet pieces.
I gaze at their dispersement
I look around and wonder -
I too feel dispersed in fragments.

**_Helen Crawford_**

# The Quiet Moment Late at Night

the quiet moment late at night
the quiet house
the short dull pause
before I quit another day

was the exact moment when I heard
the gentle entry into consciousness
the far-off, almost easily missed
can't-place-it in the dark outside—
perplexing half-remembered sound,
so far away, but near

it was!—the winter geese
calling across the dark
following patterns of stars
across a season
through a sky repeating
yet again
yearinyearout...

to reassure, confirm, check bearings
I had lost
out there by night

and, most cruelly of all
but heavy with inevitability's sinking truth
the thought came home —
yes, they are going home
which, north or south?
which is their home?
And maybe both alike are home.
it is a question without meaning

and perhaps the death I fear
and which I cannot bear
to see drag him away
from this significant street of turnings,
signs, additions, progress constantly ongoing
magnificent—gone—
no—yes—I dare at least to wonder
(in that cold dark calling into distances outside)

whether home might not be equally
somewhere out there.

### *Ruth Dunster*

# The sixth sense

*MESSAGE TO ALL SENSES.*
*Repeat. MESSAGE TO ALL SENSES.*
*Body temperature and pulse have increased by 10%.*
*Overall co-ordination reducing but stable.*
*Energy levels falling to 80% average figure.*
*Awaiting status reports. Over.*

Sight here.
We left the bathroom approximately ten minutes ago
and have returned to another section of the dance floor.
The increase in body temperature can be explained by
scantily-dressed female subject in the immediate vicinity.
Visibility is deteriorating due to poor overhead lighting
thus placing extra pressure on both the cornea and iris.
Over.

Smell here
Quite a powerful aroma has just been detected
from the subject who must be coming closer to us
Sources inform me that it could be poison or chanel.
In the bathroom cubicle, both armpits were tested
and the results are surprisingly better than I expected.
I think I can detect an alien substance to our left.
Over.

**Sound here.**
**Noise levels are quite unsatisfactory in this region.**
**I am picking up a great deal of interference from**
**one of the nearby speakers blaring so-called music.**
**We could only manage another ten minutes of this.**
**Hold on, incoming message from female subject.**
**'Do..you..come..here..often?"**
**Over.**

Touch here.
We have just made contact with the female subject.
The palms of her hands are even sweatier than ours
but we have now negotiated a close waistline embrace.
The subject appears to be impeding further progress
by returning our hands to their present position.
She is failing to imitate our embarrassing dance pattern.
Over.

Taste here.
Alcohol conshumption has thankfully shtopped
and the chewing gum has losht most of itsh flavour.
Vocal chords have not been used shince visiting the bar.
According to my recordsh, the lasht communication was:
"A pint of heavy and a packet of nuts please".
Uh oh. You should shee what he's doing now.
Over.

*Sixth sense to all other senses.*
*Doesn't he ever learn.*

### *Stephen Allan*

# Extract from "Wired to the moon"

A letter came this morning, Sarah's dead.

Her husband wrote "Sarah took her own life on the 20th October". I only met him once, he seemed nice enough. I didn't really know Sarah that well. We met last year, she was back finishing the degree she'd started years earlier. We met, we talked, swapped life stories; congratulated each other on being survivors.

Poor Sarah; marriage and university both second attempts. I wonder if her suicide was a second attempt?

She told me about the first marriage and the baby, about the periods of mental illness, the spells in hospital, the hallucinations. She even showed me the wild, beautiful poetry, written when she was someone else.

"My name is Sky"

But she didn't tell me that she wanted to die.

She was better. Recently remarried, and back to finish her degree with only the pretty pill box containing a minimum dosage to show where she had been.

She was in love. She said she no longer wanted or needed the harsh feminist texts with which I armed myself. But she believed in me. I remember her sitting on the wall outside the library, wrapped up in her big tweed coat and the red scarf that she had brought back from Moscow, laughing at my opinions on the men who inhabit academia.

"Oh Lizzie, you're brilliant. I'll see your name in print one day"

Not now.

Why Sarah? Why? If you were content in a cottage with your love?

Did Sky come back? Sky wrote mad, wild, wonderful poetry. Your husband wrote:

"Sarah graduated M.A. Arts after two resits".

And he signed the letter, the terrible letter telling me of your death:

"Cheers for now, Ian."

Sky wouldn't have been able to live with a man like that.

She was too far above him.

## *Maggie Graham*

I lie in the dark at night
I cannot sleep, I wait for light
My head is buzzing like a bee
Oh when oh when will I be free

Something happened in my childhood
I knew it was bad, he said it was good
I did not tell, so no one could hear
I was alone with all my fear

He's dead now, just as well
I hope that bastard rots in hell
I'm so happy to be me
because today, I am free

If you suspect child abuse, do say
Please, oh please, don't turn away
It may be a mistake, it may be true
But what if that child really needs you

I used to walk for miles in pain
Come sunshine, snow or rain
Hurting and crying on my own
But now I know where I'm going

Life goes on with things to do
and to myself I will be true
I won't give up, that's for sure
It was not my fault, I was pure

*Anonymous*

# Who cares?

Who cares does anyone?
Who cares about me,
Who cares, passers by
What do they see
When they look at me?
A pathetic old drunk
That stinks of cheap wine
Who cares for the life
I once knew as mine?

Do they care how I feel?
Or care if I can?
Who cares I was once
A respectable man
Who sees through the filth
To the human beneath
What do they feel
When we pass in the street?
Don't they  know I have feelings
Can they not feel my shame
Don't they know I'm addicted
I'm not really to blame
Don't they hear my mind screaming
Can't they see I cry out
For release from this torment
To my God every night.
Don't they care I'm not living
Just waiting to die
Oh why don't they care
Oh why, Dear God why?

### *I. O'N*

# Silence of speech
# on the talkative mind

In my life
I've had to endure
the unpleasant predicament
of mental hell.
With the silence of speech
on the talkative mind.
Lead to treacherous
tedious
tiresome times.
Watching, waiting
and wondering when to speak
when not to talk
to listen.

My throat tightened, and relaxed
relaxed and tightened.
Therefore, anxieties set in
and I was put in a confused
and complex state of mind.
That led me to hide
in the avenues of the enigmatic mind.

Most of these problems are behind me
there's the future to consider
and not the past.
At this moment in time
my speech is flowing
confidence that's growing
reassurance
that's being insured
with every passing year.

*Pedro Keldro*

# The Silvered Glass

Who is this stranger who watches me
Shaving his face every morning
He is balding, he peers through spectacles
Scraping his wrinkled face.

I am in my twenties, he in his fifties
My thoughts are lascivious, his of an aching back
Stooping over the wash-hand basin
My teeth are like pearls, what's left of his
Like the keys of a pub piano.

I have seen this stranger before
The old journeyman, when I was an apprentice
I have seen him playing dominoes
Or waiting in the post office
Fumbling with his pension book.

I have listened to his "I'll never forget the time" stories
Repeated time and time again
I have watched his body carried to the waiting hearse
His family looking like the actors
In an under-rehearsed play.

I have turned away from the silvered glass
I don't want to look the stranger in the eye
For the truth hurts, and I don't enjoy pain
The pain for which there is no analgesic.

### *Bill Stevenson*

# song

yi surta
keep trynti avoid it thats
thi difficult bitty it

jist
no keep findn yirsell
sitn

wotchn thi telly ur
lookn oot thi windy

that wey yi say
christ a could

go a roll n egg
ur
whuts thi time fuck me

wiv nay
cookn oil nwi need
potatoes

*Tom Leonard*

# Saturation

I'm fu, of drink, of liquid,
of images, of poisons
that I cannot name;
so light of head
beyond all reasoning.

Descending the evolutionary trail
Cromagnon Man
beating bones
in a day light
that doesn't touch me.

Shunning the light,
rejecting life.
Transient Saturation,
victim of chemistry.
Fully fat.

Consumed after consuming.
Totally obese, beyond filling.
I want emptiness!!
I want cleansing!
I want essence!

Give me the light
that doesn't fill
the light
I can swim in
without drowning.

The light that doesn't burn me
Expose me to the light of life
let it shine
on every molecule
And cast out every darkness.

***Dominic Boyle***

# Suffering Alchoholic

Rattling of keys, banging of doors
Yellow brick walls and dirty floors
Yes I'm in prison once again for my crime
Which is for drinking alcohol all the time
Breach of the peace so they say
But that's just an excuse to lock me away
I don't smoke dope, I don't take LSD
I have had cold turkey for drinking you see
It's this compulsion inside of me
It's Johnny Walker calling to me
Why won't you set me free
My hands are shaking my legs are too
I break out in a cold sweat just for you
Johnny why do you do me like you do?

Have you ever heard of Jekyll and Hyde
That's how I've been described
Split personality you see
That's the power Johnny has over me
So as I sit in my cell both dull and bright
I think about you both day and night

So if you see a man who's lost his way
Please don't mock him every day
By saying he's just a hobo anyway
Cos it could be you some day
And always remember and don't forget
Even the dull and the ignorant need to have their story

*Tommy McGinnigle*

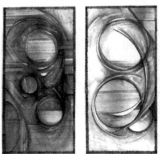

# Audience

Audience, I must pacify you
with a joke or two.
O Homer, would you have done this
in your vast synthesis
of armour and the sea.
Or Dante with his grilles of fire
would you have thrown to them
as into a sparkling flame
your squirming enemies.

*Ian Crichton Smith*

# Where Is The Left Luggage?

I carry this heavy bag around
It tires me
I don't know where to lay it down
I get no rest.

The bag contains my anger
I've had it all my life
It holds memories of my father
A violent drunk.

It also holds my fear
A timid child
And now a timid adult
Behind my shield of bravado.

I want to lay it down
To get some rest
To ease what's left of life's journey
Where is the left luggage?

**_Bill Stevenson_**

When you were
sitting at home
in your mystic silence,
listening to the future
from the telegraph-poles
of the world,

and stars told of dynasties
in their vast volume,
while radios and pianos
twinkled in the darkness,

what did you expect?

### Peter Mackie

# Ward Visitor.

*for Drew*

They said it was a glorious autumn.
Outside and fat with heat the days breathed easy
so they said.

Behind the glass, even the leaves sunburned, fit only
for shade, for bees out late, for
dying wasps.

I watched you,
open-necked across the car park
sleeves rolled and hoping for tan.

Aware of other options, other
things you could be doing, still I waited, let you drive me home.
A whole September of Saturdays, we'd
drink, fake reckless, take the same sides beneath my sheets.

Come Monday and tucked back under theirs,
I'd check my neck for crimson trophies:
a teenager again, needing proof.

When winter came, they said it was time, sent me packing.
I took my case, a month's diazepam, the shore road bus.
Too bright, too sober, much too cold; the place I called
home from habit chilled to the bone.

But it was. I was. Going on.

Now well past spring and spring again, memory returns
green without warning. Out of the blue, an Indian Summer,
gold arms in glimpses under the hospital rowans,
my eyes casting for front-door keys.

Folk tell me still how well I look. I do.
I hope that some are passing word until it reaches you.

## *Janice Galloway*

# Porcelain

Can't you see the patina
on my china skin?
I'm already cracked,
like an unfunny joke.

I'm eggshell white
with florid cheeks;
my startled blue eyes
see you, see you.

Can't you see my pretty hair?
It unravels down my back,
like poor Rapunzel's
on a less than perfect day.

If you drop me, I'll break.
Nothing new.
You can patch me up—
yes, I usually mend.

I'm porcelain  cold,
but never mind—
I sit on your shelf,
and I see you, see you.

*Anne Marr*

# Manic

I want to go mad
be a voluptuous blonde
with tits like Pamela Anderson
and a smile like Goldie Hawn.

I want to be streamlined
gyrating through space
shag the man on the moon
smear my scent all over his face.

I want to fly with a bee
watch the leprechauns pee
see goblins make pornography
show a snake my warm geography.

I want out of the ordinary
going into the voids
where creatures have missed
my bright coloured toys.

I want the tallness of Naomi Campbell
not the shortness of Donna Campbell
I want to go mad again.

**_Donna Campbell_**

# Valley of tears

Tears hot and salty flowing unrestrained
forging a path of recovery on one's face
tears suppressed a lifetime
from the eyes of one tamed
to do the deeds of one's captors
masked with evil ... monsters with names

Tears bringing relief ... comfort and sadness
to one's mind, once beyond repair
of memories, dark and unconditional
once thought of as complete madness
as one acts out the puppet on the string
but they break ... distancing badness

Tears most welcome become a waterfall
gushing out and over, thundering ...
down, down ... turning into healing waters,
soothing and calming is their effect
reflecting one's real Self
A woman strong ... proud, no longer small.

*Kathleen King*

# This bugs ma mind

1
Whit am a daen here
Jist whit am a daen here
staunin here dressed up like a fairy aff a Christmas tree
a don't want to be here, a could be at hame oot playin in the back
or watching cartoons oan the telly.

2
Whit am a daen here
Jist whit am a daen here
ma maw says,
"come oan oot" get yersel dressed an we'll away up tae the fair at Bella Park
I so a will, me walking up an doon that big hill
yur shoes full o goad knows whit
bit here a um.

3
Whit am a daen here
Jist whit am a daen here
ah mean who's interested in coos, dugs, cuddys,
they don't dae anything fur me "cartoons dae"
we canny even get a shot o' the shows
ma maw says we've nae money
ach am sick, scunnered, fed up.

4
Whit am a daen here
Jist whit am a daen here
see me, am jist gony go in the huff
a mean it am jist gony go in the huff
am gony staun here wae ma erms folded
an no speak
ach a wish a wisnae here.

5
Whit am a daen here
Jist whit am a daen here
goad this no speaking.  Its getting boring
I will huv tae think o something so a can keep ma mooth shut
whit will a think aboot
a know yon Bugs Bunny oan the telly.

## *Jim McCann*

# This Place

People of this place today
come on forward and have your say.
Don't be shy and don't hold back,
tell this place what it doth lack.

Be you black or be you white
let's make this place one of delight.
Shake each other's hand right now
and work out what to do and how.

Vandalism and violence is not the answer
to anything except disaster.
So come on put your heads together
and make this place better than better.

## *Carrie Palmer*

to have access to the silence


to feel part of the silence that is part of that which shares you and not-you
to feel not liable to be attacked at an ontological level

to sense being as not being deprived of being
to sense that it is ok, whatever the it is that is a way of describing you

to sense the it as being something that includes all of your being, from the time you were born



to sense the it as being something that includes all of your being, from the time you were born

to sense that it is ok, whatever the it is that is a way of describing you
to sense being as not being deprived of being

to feel not liable to be attacked at an ontological level
to feel part of the silence that is part of that which shares you and not-you


to have access to the silence


### *Tom Leonard*

# The waiting room

My mind races—caught in my own net of fear.
Like a fish caught I struggle to be free.
In the distance your voice calls -
But you must speak with me while I'm listening.
My own depth of pain
Swamps the pain of others.
Those faces surrounding me.
Guilt embraces this solitary time for me.
No longer can I hide my pain in yours.
Compensate a truth in your suffering.
When I'm freer I'll be one with you.
I know your pain—the ache within
To you I cannot be until I face my pain -
Deal with ache and loss.
Why do you not hear me?
I say no—I mean no.
The words I say fall on deafness.
Three sides—the curtains surround me.
One side—the endless chimney tops
Through that window.
The urge to smash the glass
Rent the curtains—
Clear the clinical pervasive
Intrusion on my body.
Judge me not as a woman
For what I cannot do -
Judge me for the woman I am
And the woman I want to be.
These dark days surround and enfold me—
A darkness not claimed—
Denied for so long
Engulfs the space within.
I hear the echo of footsteps running—
The echo of my own self running.
Knowing the darkness of pain
Ever increasing—
Can I keep my distance—
Stretch ahead—if only one more step
I'll be fine.
But two more steps and the cliff's edge...

### Helen Crawford

# The Suffering Christ

You hung there
Brown eyed
Blood dripping
From the thorns
Digging into your head.

I was taught
to imagine
how you suffered
and I was told
you suffered for me.

I couldn't grasp
what that meant.
If you suffered
for me
why did I suffer too?

**_Kay Carmichael_**

# Words? Winking?

Yesterday they tumbled in
To the room of my head
Chasing, racing, playing,
Fooling, dancing in a mindless game of tag
Rushed through, waving and shouting
Poured out, a cloudburst, a flood.

Today
The room
Is empty.

I cannot tempt them away from the corners
The curtains
The nooks and crannies
Where they have hidden
Head in hands
Deaf to my call
Refusing to play.

### *Morwyn Porter*

"NEXT!
No, No! NoT 'you

The change from
"fromp"
to
Cygnet

LIGHT.
Enter
again

TRAPPED
IN A
DARK
Room

CHILD
WITHIN

125

# The flea

I am a hungry wee flea.
I live in a flat three storeys up in the heart of the Gorbals.
There was a skinny dug and a half starved cat.
So what a chance having a feed from that lot.
Man and wife came back fae the Pub.
Hid some mer drink and jump into bed.
So did the half starved cat and skinny dug.
As they settle doon fur the night.
I started jumping aroon fae dug to cat tae man and wife.
I had a great time.
The man and wife clawed in places they didn't like.
Up in the morning for a wash and scrub.
The wife shouted to her man,

"Kick that fleahouse of a dug out!"

He opened the door.
Wae wan mighty kick and a couple of "yelps" doon the sterrs.
And we were oot in the street.
The poor mutt wandered all day and part of the rainy night.
I thought of other places to stay.
Better than on a wet dug's back awe night.
Ootside one of the posh Hotels a lady came oot.
She carried a wee French Poodle.
And another strode by her side.
I had a new pal who stayed in a toffy flat in Bearsden.
With wall to wall carpets and lots of room to play.
I met a wee French Flea.
And we are raising a family now.
They are uptoon jumping all over the place.

### E.  Flanagan

# Writing Workshop

We sit, eight of us, round four tables pushed together
the sun is shining and the air is warm
we sit, pens, pencils, biros, writing
moving constantly as we are told.

Keep writing, don't let the hand stop
don't let the mind take over
fetch the feeling
let it jump upon the page,
run about.

We sit, eight of us, round four tables pushed together
we have a unit
we are together and write together
and the energy we bring makes us
more than eight.

We are strong and powerful
We can move mountains
we can shift the boulders of the mind
shake the ground and disturb the residents
which laugh and taunt us
making us believe we cannot win.

When it's over we sit and climb out slowly
let out all the words and laugh
in wonder at ourselves.

*Morwyn Porter*

# Sunset through Clouds

**1**

I can't describe —
it's useless —
how dependent I still am,
upon your still, still calm.

Your silent light,
your waves of ribbon cloud,
the lines along your outstretched palm —
upon your still, still calm.

**II**

The same a long beginning ago —
a cold wind playing my soft young face
until calloused retrials of error,
unlearning,
can allow a slow pause full of light evening breath
with a hint of the same still, still calm.

In a circled return I see me,
me again,
at a door on the shoreline
a slow exhalation of patience
and peat-smoked salt tiredness
the bleach in my apron is rough as the tide
and I look out again.

In the Gaelic a psalm
prophesied all this calm.

### *Ruth Dunster*

# Index of Authors

# Index of Artists

# Trongate Studios
## *The Philosophy, Aims and Objectives*

In January 1994 Project Ability, the Glasgow based arts development organisation, was awarded a Specific Grant on Mental Illness to undertake a pilot project to establish an arts studio specifically for people who have experienced mental health problems. Two and a half years on, The Trongate Studios is a successful arts facility which has established itself firmly within the artistic community of the City, with over 70 people accessing the Studios up to five days per week.

In April 1996 members of Trongate Studios were invited to submit work for the Survivors' Poetry Anthology "Sweet, Sour & Serious"

The Trongate Studios aims to offer support to people who have mental health problems, through the fostering of artistic activity and the development of their creative skills as independently motivated artists, helped by the support and experience of fellow artists.

This is made possible with media specific areas for ceramics, painting, drawing, computer, textiles, photography, woodwork, printmaking, sculpture, a clean area, public gallery, canteen as well as communal work spaces and more established individual work spaces.

Project Ability employs full time professional artists who work alongside studio artists in an advisory and encouraging capacity.

The Trongate Studios also engage, on a temporary basis other professional artists to work with studio artists through a series of short term residences and workshops/master classes.

The Trongate Studios aims to be part of the comprehensive integrated Community Mental Health Service of the Greater Glasgow Area, whilst establishing itself firmly within the artistic community of the City.

18 Albion Street Glasgow G1 1LH Tel: 0141 552 2822 Fax: 0141 552 3490

Project Ability is supported by
the Scottish Arts Council
and Glasgow City Council

# Special Thanks

Special Thanks requires a long list

*Glasgow Association for Mental Health (GAMH)* who have tolerated our presence in their already overcrowded office, given us the almost exclusive use of one of their computers, access to phones, their staff helped us with our funding applications, and acted as a parent organisation in managing our first year of funding.

*The Scottish Arts Council* Combined Arts Panel for part funding our Revue and tour of Hospitals and Day Centres. The literature panel for part funding for professional writers to facilitate workshops and part funding for a feasibility study.

*Glasgow City Council* for the cost of mounting an exhibition of poetry and images at the Out of Sight Out of Mind exhibition at Kelvingrove Art Gallery, and support for our work with professional writers and performers, and the publication of this anthology.

*Greater Glasgow Community and Mental Health Services NHS Trust* for core funding to employ a development worker, administrator, sessional staff and £2,000 towards the current anthology.

*Professional writers and performers* who have worked with us including:  Janet Paisley, Gerry Loose, Kathy Galloway & Hamish Whyte (Editorial advisers), Gerrie Fellows, Mick Parkin, Ian Crichton Smith, Alison McMoreland, Margaret Fulton-Cook, Jade Reidy.  Kay Carmichael (who chaired the adhoc steering group which secured the initial one year funding).

*Survivors' Poetry Scotland Development Steering Group* who monitor and evaluate the overall work of Survivors' Poetry Scotland: John Jackson (Greater Glasgow Health Board),  Mary Troup (GAMH), Jim Eaglesham—Glasgow Advocacy Network (GANET), Anne Hawkins NHS Trust, John Alexander (Glasgow City Council Social Work), Ewan McVicar (Songwriter & Storyteller).

*Survivors' Poetry Scotland Management Group* who attend workshops and performances and carry out the ongoing tasks of Survivors' Poetry Scotland:  Donna Campbell, Dominic Boyle, Eddie Flanagan, Jack Withers, Pedro Keldro, Louise McLennan.

To Andy McLennan who designed our headed notepaper.

*Trongate Studios* Matthew Healey & Sandie Kiehlmann

*Project Ability* for a workshop room.

*Strathclyde Arts Centre* for their ongoing support in use of space.

*Margaret Blackwood Housing Association* for a workshop room.

*Centre for Contemporary Arts (CCA)* for use of their Studio Theatre.

Linda Haase for carrying out a feasibility study

Erick Valentine - Music director for performances

Elspeth Dickie - Mime and Movement director for performances

To all Survivor Poetry groups in the UK including

A big thank you to Survivors' Poetry London - especially Joe Bidder, Alison Smith, Peter Campbell & Anna Neeter.

There are probably people we have missed out who have helped us so a thank you to them.

# Survivors' Poetry UK

## *A Quality Literature and Performance Resource by and for survivors of the mental health system*

**Survivors' Poetry** is a national literature and performance resource providing workshops, performances, readings, networking and training. Founded in 1991 by four poets who have had first-hand experience of the mental health system, **Survivors'** is funded by the Arts Council of England, London Arts Board and the Mental Health Foundation. **Survivors' Poetry** has a strong reputation within both disability and mainstream arts for high quality poetry and powerful, vital performance work both within London and throughout the UK, running over 300 events a year and currently employs two part-time workers plus the input from more than ten volunteers. **Survivors' Poetry** aims to provide voices from survivors through:

The National Outreach Project (National Outreach Co-ordinator - Alison Smith)

1. Continues *to develop the formation of regional Survivors' Poetry Groups* throughout Scotland, England, Ireland and Wales.

2. Support the *existing regional Survivors' Poetry Groups* including Survivors' Poetry Scotland, Leeds, Liverpool, Manchester and Mind the Poets (Swindon).

3. Support both existing and new regional Survivors' Poetry groups through advice, information, education and training.

4. Run some 25 odd events per year (including poetry and performance workshops, performances and readings) throughout the UK in collaboration with regional survivors, local (and national) arts, mental health, local community and disabled organisations. *Survivors' Poetry* events features both survivors—established and developing performers from diverse cultures. There are 'floor spots' for survivor poets who want to try out their work in front of a knowledgeable and supportive audience.

5. The National Jamboree '96 which took place in Coventry in July 1996 was the first-ever survivor-only 3-day event which celebrated the richness and diversity of the Survivors' Poetry movement throughout the UK. There are plans for a second Jamboree in 1997.

**National Lottery Funding**—*Survivors' Poetry* received £63,000 funding from the Arts Council in March 1996. This will further support the organisation's projects with the purchase of capital equipment including computer equipment with Desktop Publishing, touring pa and lighting equipment and office furniture.

**Published Work:**

1. Published in 1992, Survivors' Poetry's first acclaimed anthology *From Dark to Light* (ISBN 1 974595 00 3) was short-listed for two book-of-the-year awards and two printings have been completely sold out. A third edition is now available.

2. Our second anthology *Under the Asylum Tree* (ISBN 874595 01 1) went out on sale in February 1995 is very much in demand; the second edition is now available.

*For Further Information about regional survivors' poetry groups please contact:*
*Alison Smith, National Outreach Co-ordinator, Survivors' Poetry, Diorama Arts Centre,*
*34 Osnaburgh Street, London, NW1 3ND.*

*Tel: 0171-916-6637 (Minicom available) Fax: 0171-916-0830*

# SURVIVORS' POETRY SCOTLAND

### POETRY WORKSHOPS AND PERFORMANCES BY AND FOR SURVIVORS OF THE MENTAL HEALTH SYSTEM

**Survivors' Poetry** aims to become a national literature and performance organisation providing workshops, performances, publications, and networking throughout Scotland. The current project, based at Glasgow Association for Mental Health, is funded by the Scottish Arts Council and the Greater Glasgow Community and Mental Health Services NHS Trust.

A "survivor" is a person with current or past experience of psychiatric hospitals, users of tranquillisers and other medication, users of counselling and therapy services, survivors of physical & sexual abuse and other survivors who have empathy with our experience.

**Survivors' Poetry Scotland** was launched in August 1995 as part of the Out of Sight Out of Mind Exhibition at Kelvingrove Art Gallery. Their programme falls into four categories:

## 1. Writing Workshops.

Day time and evening, to provide participants with an opportunity to have their work reviewed and discussed in a friendly, supportive environment; to promote the writing, reading and speaking our own words in the form of letters, poems, songs and stories; to encourage an awareness of the importance of words in our every day lives and then develop the confidence and skills to express it.

## 2. Performances and Performance Workshops.

11 performances since the launch event at the Kelvingrove Art Gallery in August 1995, including the Centre for Contemporary Arts, Southern General Hospital, Strathclyde Arts Centre, and the National Jamboree of Survivor Poetry Groups in Coventry. Workshops provide opportunities to develop presentation skills: voice projection, singing, storytelling, mime, dance and music. Some of these workshops have been facilitated by professional artists and writers funded by the Scottish Arts Council.

## 3. Publications.

To raise self-esteem, to encourage writers to take pride in completed work. In collaboration with the Trongate Studios, Survivors' Poetry Scotland is publishing an illustrated Anthology with contributions from all over Scotland. This should be in print and available by the 10th October 1996 on National Poetry Day which is also World Mental Health Day. Other publications are planned including limited edition booklets by individual writers.

## 4. Research and Feasibility Studies.

A consultant was engaged in May 1996 to carry out a feasibility study with regard to the development of Survivors' Poetry Scotland. The final report will be the basis for a 3 year business plan. The same consultant is engaged in another feasibility study into the development of a Combined Arts and Mental Health Project—to be based in the centre of Glasgow. Facilities would include a Studio Theatre, Cafe, Gallery and Workshop areas for all the Arts. A fourth year Occupational Therapy student did her research thesis (Rhyme and Reason the relationship between creative writing and Mental well being) based on her observations of a series of Survivor Poetry workshops.

If you would like our current programme please send an SAE to:

Survivors' Poetry Scotland, c/o Glasgow Association For Mental Health, Melrose House, First Floor, 15/23 Cadogan Street, Glasgow G2 6QQ.

Tel: 0141-204 2270 • Fax 0141-204 2770 • Registered Charity No. FCO 06220